D1401586

Wonders of the Bison World

SIGMUND A. LAVINE
and
VINCENT SCURO

ILLUSTRATED WITH PHOTOGRAPHS AND OLD PRINTS

DODD, MEAD & COMPANY · NEW YORK

*Dedicated to the misnamed buffalo
whose hoofs have left a lasting impression
on American history*

Frontispiece: *A plains bison in Yellowstone National Park*

Illustrations courtesy of: Jack DeLorme Photography Ltd., Calgary, Alberta, 60; Fort Niobrara Refuge, 21 *top; Harper's Weekly*, 39; Edgar T. Jones, Edmonton, Alberta, 9; National Park Service, 2, 28, 30, 38, 45, 53 *top*, 59; National Park Service Photo by William S. Keller, 21 *bottom*; St. Labre Indian School, Ashland, Montana, and Vincent Scuro, 15; Vincent Scuro, 12, 19, 25, 34, 58; State Historical Society of Colorado, 22; Smithsonian Institution, 17, 46, 49, 51 *top*; US Army Photograph, 6, 24, 27, 33, 36, 54; USDA-Soil Conservation Service, 26, 35, 37; USDA-SCS Photo by Troy N. Berry, 42; USDA-SCS Photo by Larry Goff, 61; U.S. Fish & Wildlife Service, National Bison Range, 53 *bottom*.

Library of Congress Cataloging in Publication Data

Lavine, Sigmund A
    Wonders of the bison world.

    Includes index.
    SUMMARY: Discusses the legends and lore connected
with the bison and describes its physical characteristics,
habitat, and behavior.
    1. Bison, American—Juvenile literature. [1. Bison]
I. Scuro, Vincent, joint author. II. Title.
QL737.U53L38   599'.7358   75-8732
ISBN 0-396-07146-5

Contents

1. "Such Is the Stock from Which I Spring."   7
2. Lore and Legend   13
3. Physical Characteristics   24
   General Features   24
   Size and Weight   24
   Speed and Strength   25
   Hair   26
   Coloration   27
   Head   29
4. Bison Habits   32
   Herd Life   32
   The Rutting Season   35
   Newborn Bison   36
   Food   37
   Life on the Range   38
5. "Where the Buffalo Roam"   41
6. Conservation Today   52
   Cattalo   56
   Beefalo   56
7. Hunting Bison with a Camera   57
   Index   62

Plains bison, or "buffalo," today

1

"Such Is the Stock from Which I Spring"

> Buffalo Bill, Buffalo Bill
> Never missed and never will;
> Always aims and shoots to kill
> And the company pays his buffalo bill.

This jingle, which was popular in the late nineteenth century, is only partly true. Although William Frederick Cody's skill as a hunter provided more than enough meat to feed the construction crews of the Union Pacific Railroad, he was not entitled to the nickname "Buffalo Bill." Actually, Cody did not shoot a single buffalo. The thousands of animals he killed were bison. No true buffalo has ever roamed the New World.

The earliest known ancestors of the bison lived in Asia in the latter part of the temperate period that preceded the Ice Age. Unlike many of the mammals that evolved during the preglacial era, these animals adjusted to the climatic change caused by the sheets of ice that slowly slid southward from the Arctic and covered much of the northern hemisphere. Not only did they withstand the bitter cold but also they extended their range into Europe. As they spread westward—probably in search of forage

—their size increased and their horns became larger. The fossilized skulls and horns of extinct species have enabled zoologists to trace the evolution of the bison from prehistoric times.

Because the stocky, long-horned descendant of the original bison developed on the flat, treeless plains of Russia, scientists call it the "steppe wisent" (*Bison priscus*). The steppe wisent was the first bison to live in the New World. It crossed the land bridge that connected Siberia and Alaska during the Ice Age when the waters that were to form the Bering Strait were held in suspension by masses of ice.

Its movement restricted by glaciers, the steppe wisent ranged across Alaska for centuries. Then, a brief warm period temporarily thawed the ice sheet and bands of the steppe wisent wandered southward in search of grass. There is no doubt that they found lush pastures and, as a result, became much larger than their relatives that had remained in the north. Paleontologists —students of the life of past geological periods and its relationship to living species—have excavated in Kansas the fossil remains of the largest bison ever to live on this continent. This species had tremendous horns which are the source of its scientific name, *Bison latifrons*, derived from the Latin for "wide forehead."

Latifrons became extinct as the Ice Age ended. The species was replaced by a much smaller bison (*Bison antiquus*). This animal was hunted by the first men known to live in North America and, in time, was exterminated by the primitive nomads who wandered over the Great Plains.

Although the prairies no longer supported bison, a short-horned species from Siberia that had migrated from the Old to the New World continued to roam Alaska. Known to science as *Bison bison occidentalis*, its ancestors were the steppe wisent. As the ice melted and grass took the place of glaciers, *occidentalis* trekked southward, reached the Great Plains, and, eventually,

The wood "buffalo" is also a member of the bison species. Photographed at Canada's Wood Buffalo National Park.

spread over much of North America. In the centuries that followed, *occidentalis* evolved into the animal zoologists classify as the American bison—the "buffalo" of common speech.

Legend holds that a coal-black bison known to early settlers as the "Pennsylvania buffalo" lived in the Ohio River Valley. But there is no record of any pioneer who saw this animal, said to lack a hump. Nor is there any scientific evidence that the creature ever existed. As a result, zoologists are convinced that the only place a humpless bison ever grazed was in the tall tales told along the Old Frontier.

However, all American bison are not alike. There are two recognized subspecies—the plains bison (*Bison bison bison*) and the wood bison (*Bison bison athabascae*). The latter is the larger of the two and has darker and woollier hair.

While the American bison was developing into its present-day form, true buffalo were evolving in the Old World. Like bison, these animals stemmed from the steppe wisent of Siberia. Thus the smallest of all wild cattle—the anoa of Celebes—and the powerful water buffalo of the Orient, as well as the fierce forest buffalo of Africa, are all related to the American bison. This family also includes, among others, the banteng, gayal, koupray, and yak.

But the closest kin of the American bison is the European wisent (*Bison bonasus*). Originally, there were two subspecies of wisent—the lowland wisent (*Bison bonasus bonasus*), which ranged widely over the lowlands of Europe, and the mountain wisent (*Bison bonasus caucasius*). Today, the mountain wisent is extinct—the last specimen was killed in 1925—but the lowland type has survived because of the efforts of conservationists.

At the start of the twentieth century, the only surviving wild

Old print of the European wisent, close kin to the American bison

10

wisent inhabited the Bialowieza Forest in Poland. The herd was protected by the Czar of Russia, but royal decrees meant nothing to starving peasants during the First World War. When that conflict ended, it was learned that all the wisent had been killed and eaten. Fortunately, animals from Bialowieza had been distributed to zoos throughout the world before the war, so their offspring were used to rebuild the herd.

History did not repeat itself during World War Two. Both the Russians and the Germans forbade the killing of wisent when they invaded Poland and strictly enforced their edicts. As a result, the Bialowieza herd was unharmed. After the war, Polish authorities improved its quality and increased its numbers by breeding the animals with wisent from zoos. Meanwhile, several wisent refuges were established in the Soviet Union and populated with surplus stock from Bialowieza.

Biologists and zoologists in charge of wisent reservations are trying to re-establish the lowland wisent as a free-living animal over a portion of its former territory. They also hope to reconstruct the mountain wisent. This will be a far more difficult task than was the saving of the American bison from extinction. It can only be accomplished by interbreeding animals that are the descendants of lowland wisent cows and Kaukasus, the last mountain wisent bull that is known to have survived. Although these hybrids have very few of Kaukasus' characteristics, interbreeding them may, in time, produce calves that resemble him. If so, the mountain wisent may once again forage in the upland forests of Russia.

As indicated, zoologists have deftly traced the evolution of the bison and wisent. But they have had little success in convincing the general public that it is incorrect to call an American bison a buffalo. Truth to tell, scientists themselves are often guilty of using bison and buffalo interchangeably in non-technical books and articles.

The name "buffalo," as the sign at an animal farm in New Jersey indicates, is more commonly used than the zoological term "bison."

Actually, "buffalo" was in common use long before the American bison was studied scientifically. The word comes from the English buffe or buffelo, which, in turn, derived from *les boeufs* (oxen), the name given to bison by French trappers.

The mountain men, who were more interested in beaver fur than buffalo hides, mangled *les boeufs* into "buffelow." William Clark, who kept the journal of the expedition he and Meriwether Lewis led through the unmapped West to the Pacific Ocean, either was not sure what to call the animals that grazed the Great Plains or he was a poor speller. At times he referred to "buffalow" and, at others, to "buffaloe."

Thus, for nearly two centuries, the American bison has been miscalled "buffalo." The chances are that the monarch of the grasslands will never have any other name in popular speech.

2

Lore and Legend

"Did you have any trouble driving through all them buffalo on the other side of the river?" asked the storekeeper as a customer clambered down from his wagon.

"Well, a little," was the reply. "The big 'uns didn't bother me a bit but it was a danged nuisance stopping the team every five minutes to pull calves out of the wheel spokes."

In another town, a salesman from New York City making his first selling trip across the Plains bet the clerk in his hotel that no one had ever seen 100,000 plains buffalo at one time. To settle the wager, the salesman and clerk agreed to ask the first three individuals who came into the hotel how many buffalo were in the largest herd they had ever seen.

The first man they queried disclaimed credit for encountering a large herd while riding over the prairie but remembered counting 200,000 antelope in a day. His companion also admitted he hadn't observed a tremendous number of buffalo at any time although he recalled watching a million elk feeding. When the third man to enter the lobby was approached, he said, "I've seen three million billion buffalo at one time!"

"Come on, now," chided the salesman, "that's laying it on pretty thick."

"Naw, stranger, 'tis true. When I was a boy working wagon trains, we had to corral the wagons one day to keep them from being busted by stampeding shaggies south of the Platte. Say, them critters came so fast that it took fifty men shooting day and night to split 'em. Looked like we weren't agoing to make it 'cause the guns were getting red hot, but the buffalo suddenly changed direction and we were able to hitch up and cross the Platte. When we got on the other side we found out how danged lucky we had been—looking back, we could see the main herd acoming."

These tall tales are typical of the yarns told in the West when bison grazed on the outskirts of practically every settlement. But such outlandish exaggerations must not be confused with deliberate lying. Pioneer storytellers may have stretched, strained, and hidden the truth, but it was present. Thus the first story is merely a sensational way of announcing the arrival of the calving season while the second anecdote jokingly advances the sincere belief of the frontiersman that it was impossible to count all the bison on the Plains.

Because the red man considered the plains buffalo a sacred animal, he never made it the butt of jokes as did the white man. No Indian dared to speak irreverently of it for fear of offending the Great Buffalo that ruled both the Earth and the land of spirits. The Great Buffalo was also thought to control the movements of the vast herds. As a result, members of the Flathead tribe refrained from saying anything disrespectful about bison for fear the Great Buffalo would send the herds far from their hunting grounds.

According to the Teton Sioux, Earth and the plains buffalo were one. Therefore, the Teton Sioux were convinced that if a human even whispered a disparaging remark about a live bison or bison meat, the Earth would hear it and tell the Great Buffalo.

Representation of a bison-horn headdress, from the St. Labre Indian School, Ashland, Montana

The offended diety would then punish the individual by causing him to be gored to death by an angry bull or crushed under the hoofs of a stampeding band of bison.

Not only did the Plains Indians avoid angering their bison divinities but also they honored them in various ceremonies. When a Sioux maiden reached maturity, the event was celebrated in a ritual conducted by a medicine man wearing a bison-horn headdress. This rite stemmed from the belief that the Great Buffalo was the guardian of virtue, honesty, and hospitality—the qualities most important to a woman.

While all Plains tribes revered the bison, some regarded it more highly than others. Only the Sun God outranked the plains buffalo in the long list of natural objects worshiped by the Kiowa. The Atikara who divided their world into quarters allotted the southwest quarter to the bison's guardian spirit. Even the bravest warrior held the bison's guardian spirit in awe. This is why hunters in most tribes always apologized to the spirit after killing a plains buffalo. While individual hunters sought to appease the wrath of the bison's guardian spirit, entire tribes participated in rituals designed to insure "a world in which there would always be buffalo."

But the Plains Indians did not rely solely on prayers to the Great Bull of the Prairie to guarantee a successful hunt. Blackfoot braves sang special songs to attract bison, while Pawnee warriors engaged in religious rites. The Mandan presented bowls of food to a bison skull in hopes that it would call its living relatives to join the feast. Assiniboin medicine men also employed skulls to "call" the herds. A bison skull occupied a prominent position near the entrance of every Cheyenne sweathouse, and the men smoked pipes in the bison's honor, beseeching it "to rise, invest itself with flesh, and come to life to present the tribe with meat for their kettles and skins for their lodges."

Before a bison hunt, most tribes engaged in dances that mimed the actions of the plains buffalo. Sioux dancers scraped the ground in imitation of the pawing of an angry bull, the Hidatsa waved bison tails to represent those of charging bison, and the Fox reproduced a stampede by whirling and jumping. In certain tribes only members of the bison societies—individuals who had seen supernatural bison in dreams or in visions—took part in the dances. While dancing, they wore headdresses fashioned from hair and horns. These bonnets were thought by their owners to have magical powers. However, no privately owned bison headdress was credited with as many attributes as was the Sacred Hat of the Cheyenne. Constantly guarded, this hair, bead, and horn bonnet was taken out of its decorated case only when the tribe desperately needed "big medicine."

Both Piegan men and women took part in a bison dance. To the accompaniment of rattles made of split bison hoofs strung on rawhide, they improvised the courting of the cows by the bulls. The Ma'toki dance of Blackfoot women vividly depicted a bison hunt. But no dance mimicked the activities of the plains buffalo

George Catlin's painting of the Bull Dance, held annually in the earth-lodge villages of the Mandan. Note bison skins and headdresses worn by dancers.

with such realism as the dance of Mandan men.

All bison dances were designed to lure the animals closer to an encampment and to insure a successful hunt. Sacrifices were made for the same purposes. They ranged from offerings of meat to the hide of a white bison—one of the rarest of all furs. Albino bison were considered sacred leaders of the herds and special rites were conducted whenever one was killed. Anyone who owned a white bison robe was honored by all Plains tribes. However, no tribe held albino bison in higher esteem than the Fox, whose tradition maintained that a white plains buffalo had helped one of its legendary heroes to defeat its enemy, the Sioux.

In 1805, Captain William Clark recorded in his diary the things the Mandan did "to cause the buffalow to Come near" so they could kill them. Other early observers of Indian life have also described the dances, stories, rituals, and games employed by the Indians to summon bison. But although convinced that the animals would appear in large numbers if the tribe's traditional methods of "calling" them were faithfully carried out, the red men were also practical. They made sure a herd was close by before starting a hunt.

Although the Comanche sought bison in whatever direction they saw ravens flying or a "horned toad" hopping, they also sent scouts to locate their prey. So did all other tribes. Information gathered by scouts was sent back to the tribe by signals. The Cree announced the sighting of bison by waving robes; Kutenai scouts relayed the news to one another by sign language; and the Pawnee mounted a ridge so that they could be seen. The most detailed reports were sent back by Sioux scouts. They indicated the size of a herd by riding between two points.

Because a successful hunt meant the difference between life and death to a Plains tribe, hunting by individuals was taboo. The only way the greatest possible number of bison could be killed was by a cooperative effort. Therefore, each hunt was carefully planned by a leader chosen because of his good character and managerial ability. The master of the hunt appointed a number of warriors to assist him. The duties of these "policemen" ranged from killing a barking dog that might frighten the herd to whipping any brave who did not follow orders.

After a hunt, many tribes celebrated with a dance or an elaborate ceremony. After their thanksgiving ritual, Pawnee medicine men distributed meat to the elderly who had no sons to provide them with food. Some tribes offered the heart, tongue, and other portions of the bison they had killed as sacrifices.

While butchering bison, the women set aside parts of the carcasses to make charms. The Plains Cree believed that a dewclaw amulet would turn aside bullets, and Creek women wore bison-hair garters to ward off evil spirits, while their warriors were convinced that a talisman formed from part of a bull's head would keep them from being gored.

Besides being used for fetishes, portions of the body served the buffalo doctors as medicines. Each shaman had, it was believed, visited the spirit bison while in a trance or sleeping and been taught the secrets of healing. The bison also supposedly had revealed where medicinal plants could be found.

However, a Cherokee with rheumatism did not have to consult a medicine man to know that he must not eat bison meat, touch a bison hide, or use a horn utensil. If he did, he would become as humpbacked as a plains buffalo. Nor would a Crow eat the meat of an albino bison for fear that it would turn his hair gray.

Throughout the Plains, storytellers told of the spirit bison

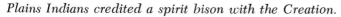

Plains Indians credited a spirit bison with the Creation.

that created the Earth. They also spun yarns in which bison married humans, helped tribal heroes outwit sorcerers, or led brave warriors into the mysterious underground world which traditionally was the bison's original home. Other stories detailed how the bison bested the coyote, legendary trickster of Indian folklore.

Buffalo Old Woman plays an important role in the myths of the Apache and she has a counterpart in the legends of all bison-hunting tribes. Some of the tales common to all Plains Indians recount the evil deeds of cannibalistic bison or tell of bison skulls that ate humans. Other narratives describe giant bison with supernatural powers that could only be killed by magic. In contrast to these gruesome accounts are dozens of stories in which kindly bison adopt an unwanted orphan and instruct him in all of Nature's secrets.

Still other tales explain the physical characteristics of the bison. The Sioux, for example, claim that, "when the world was young," Bison and Spider met on a narrow path and neither would give way to the other. When Bison threatened to stamp Spider to death, the latter wove a web over his eyes. From that time to this, say the Sioux, bison have been nearsighted.

Like the bison that once were as "numerous as the locusts of Egypt," the men who hunted them have vanished from the prairie. As a result, the dances, songs, and rituals employed by the red men of yesteryear to lure the herds are known to but a few of their descendants. Moreover, the storytellers who kept alive the oral traditions of the Plains tribes have been replaced by such modern sources of entertainment as motion pictures, radio, and television.

Nevertheless, the hoofs of the thundering herds have left their mark. For example, a plains buffalo appears on the seal of the

Bison survive today through the efforts of conservationists. A herd (above) on the Fort Niobrara Refuge, Nebraska; (below) in the Theodore Roosevelt National Memorial Park, North Dakota.

Department of the Interior. Coin collectors prize uncirculated "buffalo" nickels and avidly seek specimens of the ten dollar bill that depict Pablo, a bull formerly exhibited in the National Zoo in Washington, D.C. Pablo is also of interest to philatelists—he appears on a stamp issued in 1923.

Bison also stampede through literature and art. Library shelves are packed with books dealing with the "buffalo culture" of the Plains tribes and with the accounts of the hide hunters. Modern Indian artists, drawing on their imaginations and knowledge of ancient ways, are painting their ancestors "calling" and hunting the plains buffalo with almost the realism of

This bison sketch by an unknown artist appears on a brochure published by the State Historical Society of Colorado.

The bison is the symbol of pro football's Buffalo Bills.

George Catlin who sketched these activities over a century ago.

Today, partners at square dances are swung to the tune of "Buffalo Gal," while antique lovers pay high prices for a piece of "Westward Ho," a pattern glass decorated with the raised figures of an Indian and a bison.

Idiomatic speech also commemorates the plains buffalo. A stingy person is said to "pinch a nickel until the buffalo drips blood." Individuals who realize that they have been bluffed by an opponent admit they were "buffaloed." This slang expression probably originated from the similarity in sound between "bluff" and "buffalo."

Finally, every autumn, football fans are reminded of the powerful animals that tore up the ground when annoyed and charged anything that attempted to block their passage when they watch the Buffalo Bills. This team proudly displays a plains buffalo on its helmets.

3

Physical Characteristics

GENERAL FEATURES

Zoologists classify all living things according to similarities in physical characteristics. They have placed bison in the Order Artiodactla—the classification for even-toed, cloven-hoofed animals. Like domestic cattle, bison have two toes on each foot and an equal distribution of weight on each toe.

Within the Order Artiodactla, bison belong to the suborder Rumantia, which consists of animals that rework their food by cud-chewing. All cud-chewers have multichambered stomachs, and a bison's stomach has four chambers.

SIZE AND WEIGHT

The bison is the largest land animal on the North American continent, with a fully grown adult weighing between 700 and 3000 pounds. Bison bulls generally weigh twice as much as cows and are also more muscular.

Most bison measure between seven and twelve feet in total length, including over a foot of tufted tail. They stand between five and six feet tall at the hump, which is a prominent feature of both the wood and plains bison. The hump is formed by an

Like domestic cattle, bison are cloven hoofed with two toes on each foot.

elongation of the backbone's first ten spines and an extension of the last spinal vertebra.

SPEED AND STRENGTH

All bison have tremendous agility and can change direction easily without losing balance. Their powerful leg muscles enable them to gallop at speeds up to thirty-five miles per hour for more

The hump is one of the bison's most prominent physical characteristics.

than fifteen miles at a time. They have the strength and stamina to climb to heights of up to twelve thousand feet.

Bison are also excellent swimmers, except in icy waters where chunks of floating ice hinder their movements. Being hoofed animals, bison cannot grasp the ice to pull themselves out of the water. As a result, many bison drown each year during the spring thaw.

HAIR

Hair, one of the most important features of the bison, protects the skin and keeps the animal warm in cold weather. The body is covered with a thick hairy mat of varying lengths, the shortest growth occurring on the hindquarters. A shaggier growth two to five times thicker appears on the hump, back, and shoulders. The longest hair grows in a thick, dark mantle on the head, neck, and forelegs. In the case of the adult male bison, a beard of up to twelve inches in length may hang beneath the chin. (The hair on a wood bison's chin and forehead is much longer

Bison in the Wichita Mountains Wildlife Refuge, Oklahoma, have heavy coats to protect them in the winter.

Bison have a ragged appearance when they shed in the spring.

and finer than on the plains variety.) A bison's coat is heaviest on the hump, back, and shoulders, which makes it appear that the front half of the body contains the animal's total strength. However, the hindquarters are by no means as weak as they look.

Each spring, the thick winter coat is shed, the hair coming off in patches so that the bison has a ragged appearance. By the end of the summer, chunks of hair remain on the front part of the body but the hindquarters are almost completely hairless. With the cool weather of late autumn, the animal grows a new coat to be ready for the cold winter ahead.

COLORATION

Tiny granules of pigment known as melanin cause the coloration of a bison's hair, skin, and eyes. Most bison are born with an orange-reddish coat, or pelage, which gradually darkens to a deep brown in adulthood and may have a yellowish tint during the winter due to bleaching from the sun's rays. Occasionally, bison are born gray, yellow, or cream colored, and there are

27

This calf, from the herd at Wind Cave National Park, South Dakota, is just beginning to grow its horns.

records of black, blue, mouse-colored, piebald, and white adult bison.

The pure white bison—*bice-itse*, to the Crow Indians—is actually an albino caused by the complete absence of melanin. An average of six albino bison are born annually in the United States and Canada. Few survive the first year, although one, called Big Medicine, lived for twenty-six years on the National Bison Range in Montana.

HEAD

SKULL. A bison has a massive head with a skull that is virtually impenetrable at the forehead. The skullbone is covered with more than two inches of heavy skin, reinforced by the long mat of dense hair. The layers of bone, hair, and skin form a tough plate and provide ample protection for the brain.

Both male and female bison have sharp, curved horns, located one on each side of the head. These horns are hollow and permanent, and are formed above a bony core that extends from the skull's frontal bone. Horns average from twenty-two to twenty-six inches in length, with a thirty-inch span. On a calf, the horns are only black stubs about two inches long. Gradually, however, horns reach their full length, slowing in growth with adulthood.

The horns of an adult bull in his prime are smooth and sharp. But it is not unusual to see a deformed or cracked horn. Bison love to rub their horns against trees and stones, and, as a result, the horns are worn flat or chipped, especially on older bulls.

EYES. A bison's eyes seem to peer from shallow wells located on each side of the head. All bison (except albinos) have brown eyes, and each eye has a pear-shaped iris. Bison vision is poor— in fact, it is inferior to that of most other animals. If an object remains motionless, a bison may not see it at all.

The bison's massive skull protects its head.

EARS. To compensate for poor vision, the bison has an extremely acute sense of hearing. Its ears are located behind the horns and gather sounds for the tremendously sensitive internal hearing organs, which can distinguish the pitch, rhythm, and tonality of extremely weak and distant sounds, as well as the sounds of the bison "language."

MOUTH. Bison communicate with several distinct sounds. A snort, produced by forcing air through the nostrils, is a threatening sound. So are grunts and bellows, the growling noises created by the larynx. Bison also signal each other by grinding their teeth to produce a high-pitched sound virtually undetectable by human ears, but the bison's thirty-two teeth are primarily used for nibbling grass and chewing it.

The outer lips are black in color, while the inner lips have a bluish-purple tinge. The tongue is used for tasting food and is long enough to touch the nostrils.

NOSE. The nose is big, broad, and black, with large nostrils, and has six nasal passages as compared to four in domestic cattle. A bison's sense of smell is extremely acute. These animals can distinguish between a horse and a horse with a rider at a distance of over a mile, provided the wind is blowing their way.

4

Bison Habits

HERD LIFE

Bison are gregarious animals—they form herds simply to enjoy each other's company. Today's plains bison herds average around two hundred animals. Since wood bison and wisent inhabit forested areas where open space is limited, their herds are smaller, numbering from six to forty animals.

Life in a bison herd has both advantages and disadvantages. During cold weather, bison huddle together for warmth. They also protect each other from their natural enemies, wolves and cougars. On the other hand, the entire herd suffers when there is a shortage of food. Disease also spreads quickly through the herd, as does panic, which leads to stampedes.

Many stampedes develop so quickly it is impossible to determine the cause. The leader, generally a bull with imitative followers, senses danger, panics, and runs off. The rest of the herd, bunched closely, follows. As the sound of grinding hoofs builds to a continous rumble, a cloud of dust encircles the herd. Stampeding has its dangers. By blindly following the leader over the side of a cliff, thousands of bison have perished in a single stampede.

Bison form herds simply to enjoy each other's company.

The bison's temperament is best described as unpredictable. One minute a bison may appear serene and calm—the next, its huge frame is barreling forward with the speed and power of a small truck. At one buffalo ranch in Utah, horses were used to herd the bison until several horses were severely gored. The ranch owner replaced the horses with light pickup trucks, and the trucks were also gored!

Bison are curious animals. They habitually explore objects they have never seen or touched before. An unfamiliar object is approached with caution, the animal's eyes and ears focused on it with steady concentration. Once the object is within reach, a bison may even touch it with his tongue or nose. If fear wins out over curiosity, a bison may turn and run. But bison are by no means cowards. When backed into a corner, a bison will hoist his tail, paw the ground, bellow aloud, and charge.

All bison enjoy wallowing. When a bison wallows, he lies on

Bison have worn paint off the side of this barn by rubbing against it. They also scratch themselves on the logs in the foreground.

the ground, stretches out, rubs his head back and forth, and kicks up dust with his hoofs. This covers the animal with a layer of dust while creating an oval-shaped depression in the ground about ten feet wide.

Bison delight in scratching, especially in the spring, since this relieves the itching of their heavy coats while keeping them well groomed. A bison will rub against trees, rocks, stumps, even other bison. In fact, when the first telegraph wires were strung across the Great Plains, herds of bison rubbed so hard against the poles they knocked them over. The telegraph company tried to remedy this by driving sharp metal spikes into the lower portions of the poles, hoping to discourage the bison. Instead, the spikes only served to provide better back scratchers.

THE RUTTING SEASON

Bison bulls and cows mate during what zoologists refer to as the rutting season. This lasts from the beginning of July to the end of September, although bison in captivity have been known to mate at any time during the year.

Occasionally, two bulls pursue the same cow. When this happens, the rivals roar and bellow at each other or kick up dust from their wallows. A bull may also stand perfectly still to display his lack of fear for his opponent. These maneuvers are actually bluffs. Neither animal *really* wants to fight because fighting uses up the energy needed for rutting. When a bull avoids a fight, he also prevents possible injury.

If bluffing fails, head to head combat erupts. The opponents lock horns and wrestle until the weaker bull submits, with the winner free to court the cow of his choice, so long as *another* bull hasn't stolen her while he was busy fighting.

A bison bull standing in his wallow

A bison cow with her calf

NEWBORN BISON

Some cows breed either as yearlings or as two year olds, but most begin breeding during the third year and bear a calf every year until they are twenty-five years old. The gestation period lasts for approximately nine months, and an actual birth takes an hour or two. Each year, slightly more females are born than males.

A buffalo cow generally bears her calf during the spring. When the single calf is born (twin births are extremely rare), its eyes are open. The hump is not fully developed at birth, so baby bison strongly resemble the calves of domestic cows. A bison calf generally weighs from thirty to seventy-five pounds at birth.

Within a few hours after birth, a calf is able to follow its mother around, and it remains with her for almost a year. By the end of the first year, a calf leaves its mother to graze and frolic with the rest of the herd.

FOOD

Bison are grazers and rely on the natural grasses of their range for nourishment. "Buffalo" grass (*Buchloe dactyloides*) is a staple of their diet as is a variety of other wild grasses. Bison often eat forage plants such as vetch and pea vine, but rarely shrubs or leaves. Hay, concentrated feed, and biscuits are the mainstays of bison in captivity.

On a typical day, a bison herd begins to feed at daybreak. The herd spreads out while eating, each animal claiming its own feeding area. Bison generally graze until late morning, then lie in the sun and chew the cud. They eat again in the late afternoon and may make a trip to the nearest waterhole or salt lick.

When the ground is snow covered, a bison feeds by first clear-

Bison herd grazing on bluestem grasses in Oklahoma

Bison use their heads like plows to dig through snow for food.

ing a path through the snow with his head, then eating all the grass he has uncovered. This eating process wears off the hair on a bison's head so that a bald spot is noticeable in the spring.

The wisent's diet differs from that of the plains and wood bison. Wisent are browsers that nibble at the tender shoots of shrubs, bushes, and trees. They also eat wild berries and acorns. In the fall, when acorns are abundant, wisent may eat nothing else.

LIFE ON THE RANGE

Bison share their rangeland with a variety of living creatures —some friendly, some not so friendly.

Squirrels and gophers mingle easily with them, as do moose, elk, and bighorn sheep. The pronghorn, a handsome, fleet-footed animal often mistaken for the antelope, grazes side by side with bison in many national parks.

Insects are a nuisance for bison. Botflies and ticks burrow their way into a bison's hair and add to the itching misery of the spring "molt." The "buffalo bird"—a cowbird, actually—spends hours feeding on insects in the bison's hair and on the ground. Buffalo birds also use the bison's back as a woolly perch.

Bison herds affect the lives of many smaller range inhabitants. Wallows fill with water, becoming homes for toads and aquatic insects. Sadly, some wallows destroy the underground colonies that prairie dogs build.

Buffalo dung—the bison's solid waste—serves as a home for bugs, worms, and larvae. It is also a good fertilizer. Moreover, nineteenth century inhabitants of the Great Plains used hardened dung—buffalo chips—in place of firewood.

As noted, wolves and cougars are the bison's natural enemies. Aware of their strength in size and numbers, bison tend to ignore wolves unless provoked or attacked. A single bison bull can withstand an assault by six or seven wolves at one time.

Bison dung—"buffalo chips"—was used for fuel on the Great Plains. Note the skull beside the travellers' fire.

39

Old print shows a fight between a bison and a grizzly bear.

Cougars also prey upon bison, but only attack old cows and calves that stray from the herd. Even then, cougars stand little chance of overcoming their quarry.

Kodiak and grizzly bears are the only animals capable of killing a bison in one-to-one combat, and they do so rarely. A grizzly bear can break a bison's neck with a single swipe of its paw. Kodiak bears are even stronger than grizzlies. But a bison still holds the advantage in a fight because of its speed, agility, and charging power. In prime condition, "a bison can best any foe."

5

"Where the Buffalo Roam"

Until comparatively recent times, anyone who wanted a "home where the buffalo roam" could have built a house practically anywhere in North America. Bison formerly grazed along the eastern coast from Florida to New York, from the Atlantic seaboard westward to California, and from Canada southward to New Mexico. But the largest population of bison inhabited the Great Plains.

Actually, no one knows how many bison lived on the prairie during the exploration and settlement of the New World. Estimates vary from thirty to seventy million head. Therefore, it is easily understood that the chronicles of the conquistadors, journals of missionaries, diaries kept by travelers and traders, and the dispatches of Army officers assigned to survey the West are filled with reports of buffalo herds that "blackened the country."

Traditionally, Hernan Cortez was the first white man to see an American bison. The conqueror of Mexico supposedly examined a captive specimen in 1519 while visiting the private zoo of Montezuma, the Aztec emperor. According to historian Antonio Rivadeneyra, Cortez claimed the animal was ". . . a wonderful

Bison grazing in Texas, where Cabeza de Vaca reported seeing "oxen" with "little hornes" in 1533.

composition of divers Animals: it has crooked Shoulders, with a Bunch on its Back like a camel; its Flanks dry, its tail large, and its Neck cover'd with Hair like a Lyon. It is cloven-footed, its Head armored like that of a Bull. . . ."

Despite this vivid description, Cortez never said that he had seen a bison. The only reference to the one in Montezuma's zoo was made by Rivadeneyra, who lived his entire life in Spain. As Rivadeneyra recorded Cortez's exploits more than a century and a half after the Aztec Empire was destroyed, it is doubtful that Cortez ever saw a "Mexican Bull."

The first European definitely known to have seen a plains buffalo is Cabeza de Vaca. He tells of encountering "oxen" with "little hornes . . . and very long haires" in his account of exploring Texas in 1533. But De Vaca cannot be credited with being the first to describe bison in print. He did not publish his book until 1555. Two years previously, Gonzalo de Oviedo detailed the appearance of the "Cows of the Land to the North" in a multivolumed work dealing with the West Indies.

One of the best early descriptions of the American bison was written by Castaneda, the chronicler of Coronado's futile quest for the fabled Cities of Gold:

> . . . These cows are like those of Castile, and somewhat larger, as they have a little hump on their withers, and they are more reddish, approaching black; their hair, more than a span long, hangs down around their horns and ears and chin, and along the neck and shoulders like manes. . . .

By the time daring individuals were seeking fur, gold, and rich land in the West, knowledge of the physical features of the American bison was practically world-wide. But the multitude of the animals seen feeding on the grasslands still astonished those who crossed the Great Plains.

There was good reason. Some herds were so large that they took a week to pass a given point. At times, travelers reported, the entire countryside "appeared one mass of buffaloes." It was not unusual for trains to be held up for hours while bison ambled across the rails. Besides disrupting railroad schedules, plains buffalo swimming from one bank to another frequently forced Missouri River steamboats to drop anchor. Not only was it almost impossible to ram a vessel through the mass of swimmers but also any captain who attempted to do so was apt to find that so many of the animals had become entangled in his boat's paddle wheels that the wheels would not turn.

Although scientists have a tremendous amount of information about ancient bison, they cannot definitely answer a question about the herds that roamed the Great Plains in modern times. The query that stumps them is: Did the plains buffalo engage in seasonal migrations?

Frontiersmen were positive that the great herds moved southward at the approach of winter and turned northward as the snow melted. Some early observers insisted that Canadian plains buffalo spent the cold months in Texas and summered in Saskatchewan. But modern research has revealed that it would take the animals nearly five months to make the 1400-mile journey from Canada to Texas and almost five months to retrace their trail. This would leave them less than three months for ". . . savoring the lush forage at both ends. And even this period would be lost altogether if travel speed dropped below . . . eight miles a day."

Nevertheless, William Hornaday, the zoologist who played a most important role in saving the American bison from extinction, believed it migrated. He claimed that in the fall each herd drifted south a few hundred miles and "wintered under more favorable circumstances."

Strangely enough, the obvious flaw in Hornaday's statement was overlooked for years. If all the herds changed their range as he believed, only the southernmost one would find an abundance of grass. All the others would end their journeys in a grazed-over area recently vacated by a herd which, in turn, had taken over the pasturage of bison that had migrated south.

There is no doubt that the plains buffalo were constantly on the move. However, the evidence is strong that they did not travel along well-defined routes—except when going to water—but wandered in all directions throughout the year. We do know that certain herds sought shelter from the howling blizzards that blanketed the plains with snow. These animals left the open prairie and wintered in the sparse stands of trees that bordered the rivers running through their ranges. The most unusual of these short seasonal migrations was that made by the bison in western Canada. Instead of going south to avoid the cold, they went north—the only direction in which they could find trees.

When bison herds roved the Plains, some of them took shelter from approaching storms by heading into the trees. A herd in Yellowstone today.

If bison had changed ". . . their Country according to the Seasons of the Year," the Plains Indians would not have been nomads. They would have lived in permanent camps located along migration routes and killed the bison as they passed. It was because the sea of plains buffalo ebbed and flowed across the prairie and did not follow well-marked channels that the Plains Indians were forced to wander widely in search of game.

The bison, favorite prey of the Plains Indians, furnished not only food, clothing, and shelter but also materials to fashion hundreds of articles ranging from jewelry to shrouds. "On the western plains the buffalo and the Indian were linked as closely as they would be later on a nickle coin."

Bison meat was the staple food of the Plains tribes. Hunters immediately ate certain entrails and the liver raw, seasoning them with bile to improve the flavor, just as today we smear mustard on a hot dog. Fresh meat was roasted or stewed, bones

Catlin painted this band of Sioux encamped on the upper Missouri after a successful hunt. The women are dressing the robes. Note racks of drying meat.

were boiled in soup, and the blood was used to make puddings. Surplus meat was cached in underground pits, cut into strips and hung on poles to dry, or made into pemmican. While sun-dried meat which is called "jerky" would keep for three years without spoiling, pemmican remained edible almost indefinitely. While the method of making pemmican varied from tribe to tribe, fundamentally, the process consisted of pounding jerky into bits, mixing it with hot marrow fat, and packing the meat into airtight sacks of bison hide. One variation of the basic recipe called for the addition of wild cherries or berries.

Faced with starvation, some tribes would cut strips from bison hides to make broth. But with the exception of the Cheyenne, who baked fresh hides after removing the hair, the majority of Plains Indians considered hides unappetizing and never ate them unless desperate for food.

Everything the bison-hunting tribes wore from moccasins to false hair came from the bison. Winter clothing was made from hides tanned with the hair on, summer dress from depilated hides. Hair was not scraped off pelts used for the robes that served braves as overcoats in winter and as raincoats in stormy weather. During the cold months, robes were worn with the hairy side next to the body; when it rained, they were reversed. Pelts were also used for beds and bedding.

Hides provided the "canvas" on which Indians painted tribal records or recorded their exploits. As many as twenty hides were needed to cover the characteristic Plains dwelling, the tepee. Rawhide (untanned skin) was employed to make a wide variety of articles ranging from bridles to boats.

Space does not permit a complete listing of all the items the Plains Indians manufactured from the bison. They wasted nothing—bones became tools, toys, and toboggans; sinew, thread; internal organs, containers; horns, arrowheads and utensils; teeth, ornaments; hair, earrings and blankets. Perhaps the most unusual of these articles was the hairbrush used by Crow women, manufactured from the rough side of the bison's tongue.

Motion pictures and television have given many people the impression that the Plains Indians always hunted bison on horseback. Actually, they killed far more animals by other methods. For example, instead of galloping after a band of bison, the hunters enclosed it with a ring of fire and slaughtered the frightened beasts as they huddled together.

The two most common hunting techniques were the surround and impounding. In the surround, a group of men encircled the bison, forcing them to mill about until the weary animals became easy targets. Impounding was more complicated, its success depending upon the Indians' skill in keeping their prey moving toward a corral at the end of two fences which narrowed in like a capital **V**. Usually, the hunters drove the animals between the fences and prodded them into the corral by waving blankets and shouting. But sometimes the bison were lured into the pound by an Indian covered with the skin of a calf. Bleating as if in danger, the Indian would crawl toward the trap. The adult bison, seeking to aid the youngster, followed. When they were trapped, the masquerader ran to the fence and leaped over it to safety.

The Indians also bagged bison as the animals crossed streams, became bogged down in swampy areas, or floundered in snow. Sometimes the Indians caused a herd to stampede over a cliff. During the winter months, bison were hazed onto the ice and shot as they slipped and skidded.

After the Plains Indians acquired mounts, most surrounds were made on horseback. While this proved to be the most effective of all bison-hunting techniques, it did not give individual hunters the chance to display their skills as riders and marksmen the way chasing a galloping bison on horseback and killing it with a single arrow did. Difficult as this feat was, most Plains braves accomplished it with ease. Astride a fleet "buffalo runner" —a well-trained horse that needed no guidance—a hunter would pick out a particular bison in the herd, pursue it, and, when abreast of it, shoot it through the heart. As the Indian shot, his horse immediately lunged to one side to avoid crashing into the falling bison.

However, the white man was the bison's greatest foe. "Buffalo robes" were an important item in the fur trade—1,999,870 robes were shipped down the Mississippi to New Orleans in 1828— and thousands more were sent to other trading centers.

An Assiniboine running a Buffalo.
Drawn by an Assiniboine warrior
and hunter. Fort Union. Jan. 16. 18 57.

A "buffalo runner" was a horse trained by the Indians to pursue the bison without guidance from the rider.

As the railroads pushed westward, "sportsmen" thronged excursion trains whose agents promised that "buffaloes would be near enough to be shot from the cars." Most of the animals slaughtered on these junkets were left to rot. So were the majority of the kills made by the professional hide hunters. Although a few of the professional hunters supplied bison meat to wholesalers, most of them discarded everything but the pelt. Seeing this wanton waste, even peaceful Plains tribes began to resent the presence of the white man in their traditional hunting grounds.

In the early days of the fur trade, a prime bison hide brought about five dollars. While pelts reached a high of eight dollars just before the great herds were exterminated in the early 1880's, the average price was less than two dollars. But if the value of the hides varied over the years, there was a steady demand for them as long as they were available—no horse-drawn vehicle was comfortable in winter unless driver and passengers were bundled in a "buffalo robe." Bison pelts also kept

49

pedestrians warm. One could ". . . buy a beautiful fur-robe over-coat, well-made and lined with flannel . . ." for ten dollars.

Not all the robes stacked in warehouses in St. Louis, St. Paul, and other fur markets in the heyday of the hide hunters came from bison shot by white men. Traders bartered with the Plains tribes for pelts wherever bison roamed. Both the professional hunters and the red men were convinced that the bison herds could not be destroyed. To be sure, the animals in a certain area might be killed off, but all the pursuers had to do was move to a new hunting ground.

Then, in 1871, a process was developed that transformed bison hide into excellent leather. This invention meant the end of the vast herds. Armed with improved rifles, the hide hunters slew millions of bison. Alarmed, the Indians sought to stop them by treaties with the Great White Father. But these agreements were ignored and, as a result, the Plains became a bloody battle-field.

Despite the danger of being scalped, the hide hunters con-tinued to decimate the herds. Millions of bison carcasses decom-posed on the prairies, while the number of bison rapidly dropped. Meanwhile, some western states passed laws forbid-ding leaving any "flesh to spoil." The Congress passed a similar bill in 1871, but this did not stop hide hunting. Stronger legisla-tion was proposed in the years that followed but was consistently voted down.

By 1889 there were less than one hundred free-ranging bison in the United States. Five years later the Federal Government passed a law protecting bison. Although this edict was far too late, it paved the way for the organization of the American Bison Society in 1905. Drawing on public and private zoos and the small band of bison in Yellowstone National Park, the Society stocked refuges, where the animals thrived and multiplied. By 1915, the Society was able to report to its members that "the future of the species now seems assured."

Many white men decimated the herds for sport and profit. An old print.

Indians hunted with bows and lances, taking only what they needed to survive. Oil by Catlin.

6

Conservation Today

The great herds of buffalo that once blanketed the North American continent are gone forever. But the bison is far from extinct. Today, thanks to conservation programs in the United States and Canada, over fifty thousand bison thrive in zoos, parks, ranches, and wildlife refuges. This number is increasing so rapidly that herds must be reduced every year to maintain the balance between the number of animals and the ability of their rangeland to support them.

Every October, cowboys on the National Bison Range near Moiese, Montana, drive the park's herd in from the hills for a week-long roundup of counting, branding, weighing, and inoculation. Once corralled, the bison calves are cut out of the herd, counted, and branded on the hip with a year mark from a hot iron. The hair on the hip must be clipped short first so the brand can burn the hide. After branding, the calves rejoin the adult bulls and cows for weighing and inoculation. When this has been completed, the entire herd is released to graze in the park's pastures.

At the National Bison Range, a deferred rotation system is used to prevent park bison from overgrazing the existing range-

The bison roundup is an annual event at Theodore Roosevelt National Memorial Park, North Dakota.

Once they are brought in from the hills, bison are driven into corrals by cowboys. This is the October roundup at the National Bison Range.

Bison at Fort Riley, Kansas, wear ear tags for identification.

Two plains bison grazing in the main post corral at Fort Riley.

land. The range is divided and the herd grazes a different section every three months. This allows the natural grasses to improve in quality because every year during the growing season the herd grazes a different pasture.

The rangeland at Custer State Park, South Dakota, has enough forage to support 1,450 bison. Each year, it is necessary to remove about five hundred animals to keep the herd within the carrying capacity of the range. About two hundred are slaughtered, the rest auctioned live to nearby ranchers. Many ranchers who once raised bison as a hobby are now selling the animals commercially.

One proposal for the use of surplus bison from America's national parks includes distribution to Indians who live on reservations. The meat is an excellent source of protein, and when compared to the meat of domestic cattle is higher in essential amino acids and lower in cholesterol and saturated fatty acids.

Today there are hundreds of small bison herds in the United States. The twenty-two bison at Fort Riley, Kansas, have names like Sinbad and Crooked Horn, and wear ear tags for identification. They receive special treatment from a veterinarian who feeds them hay twice a day and also supplies a treat of cracked corn. Every six months, they are examined and inoculated for disease.

Most of the bacterial and nutritional diseases that once threatened the bison species are now controlled through systematic programs of vaccinations and proper diet maintained by the National Park Service. Many of the untreatable ills, such as cancer and tuberculosis, are not of major concern to the survival of the species.

The Canadian Department of Indian and Northern Affairs has instituted several conservation programs in Wood Buffalo National Park, located near Fort Smith in the Northwest Territories. Every two weeks, park officials conduct a bison survey from two Cessna aircraft flying at an altitude of one thousand feet. It takes eight hours' flying time to cover the park, but many bison are not countable since tall trees often block visibility from the air.

By a special treaty, Canadian Indians of Cree and Chipewyan descent are allowed to hunt the surplus bison that roam outside Wood Buffalo National Park. This hunting is not confined to any specific season but is strictly regulated by the Canadian Department of Indian and Northern Affairs.

CATTALO

As early as 1598, Captain Vicente de Zaldivar, a Spanish explorer, proposed "el catalo" in order to obtain a beef animal with the good meat qualities of domestic cattle and the rugged range hardiness of bison. But the first actual crossbreeding did not take place until 1750 in the Carolina colonies. More recently, from 1958 to 1964, the Canadian Department of Agriculture conducted intensive cattalo experiments in Wainwright, Alberta. The Wainwright Experiments, as they are known, provided extensive information on cattalo breeding but failed to produce a breed capable of reproducing itself.

BEEFALO

In 1974, a breeding developer named Bud Basolo of Tracy, California, exhibited the first beefalo, a product of more than seventeen years of trial-and-error breeding.

According to Mr. Basolo, beefalo graze on grass like buffalo and produce a beef that is higher in protein and lower in fat than that of domestic cattle. Since beefalo do not feed on grain as cattle do, their meat will be less expensive once enough are bred for commercial distribution.

7

Hunting Bison with a Camera

Want to hunt bison with a camera? If you have the time, you can enjoy some exciting "shooting" while taking a closer look at North America's largest land animal. You will find bison in zoos, animal farms, private ranches, parks and wildlife refuges in the United States and Canada. In fact, bison now live in areas where they never lived before, such as the Hawaiian Islands.

To begin your "hunt," you'll need a camera and plenty of film. Most cameras with a lens opening, focus, and shutter speed that are preset will do, but if you have a camera with adjustable focus and interchangeable lenses, bring along a light meter and a telephoto lens for close-ups.

Zoos and animal farms are the safest places to "hunt" bison since your quarry is fenced in for your protection. Of course, you won't be able to take pictures of an entire herd, but you will be able to study the bison close up in a relatively quiet setting. The best time to photograph bison is in the morning or late afternoon since these are their most active periods. Check with your local zoo or animal farm for opening and closing dates and times.

For those who want to photograph the larger herds, there are

Bison are best photographed at animal farms because they are fenced in for your protection.

several parks in the United States that offer tremendous photographic opportunities.

Moiese, Montana's, National Bison Range has a nineteen-mile self-guided tour road and a big game pasture near range headquarters. The park is open all year round; the tour road only during the summer months of June, July, and August.

Yellowstone National Park, Wyoming, has a bison population of mixed wood and plains types. Only a few bison are visible from the park's paved roads during the summer months, but horseback tours through the back trails can be arranged at park headquarters. An occasional bison can be seen near Old Faithful during the month of June.

Custer State Park, near Hermosa, South Dakota, has one of the largest bison herds in America and an eighteen-mile Wild-

One of three bison herds you can photograph while on a horseback tour through Yellowstone National Park.

life Loop Road (ten miles surfaced, eight miles good gravel) that enables you to photograph bison from your automobile. While you are in the area, you can travel a few miles south to photograph the bison herd at Wind Cave National Park, located just outside Hot Springs, South Dakota.

If you are hardy enough to leave the safety of your automobile (and do this only in parks where it is permitted), approach bison with caution. Always plan an escape route. When you are all set to take pictures, position yourself near a tree with low branches and be ready to climb it if you have to. If a bison *does* corner you, don't try to outrun him—you won't be able to. Instead, stand perfectly still and wait until he goes away. (He'll leave when he gets hungry.) Then return to your car as quickly as possible. Most park rangers suggest you remain in your car

Canada's famous Calgary Stampede features buffalo riding as one of many exciting rodeo events.

whenever bison are present.

If you prefer to photograph bison from the comfort of a grandstand seat, Canada's famous Calgary Stampede, held each year during the first two weeks of July, features buffalo riding as one of many exciting rodeo events. "The Greatest Outdoor Show on Earth" is a camera treat for anyone who enjoys Western excitement.

This is just a sampling of the outstanding photographic opportunities in the United States and Canada. So why not take the time to discover the wonders of the bison world that are waiting to be captured on film?

Good hunting!

Saved from extinction, bison graze in a national park in Tennessee.

Index

Alaska, 8
American Bison Society, 50
Apache, 20
Assiniboin, 16
Atikara, 15

Basolo, Bud, 56
Beefalo, 56
Bering Strait, 8
Bialowieza Forest, 11
Bison
  albino, 17-18, 19, 29
  "calling," 15-17, 18
  chips, 39
  classification, 24
  communication of, 31
  conservation, 11, 50, 52, 55
  evolution, 7-10
  food, 37, 38
  herds, 32
  hunting, 15-16, 18-19, 47-50
  in art, 22-23
  in folklore, 9, 13, 14
  in idiomatic speech, 23
  in legend, 19-20
  in literature, 22
  in music, 23
  in religion, 14-16, 19

Indians and, 14-18, 20, 45-48, 55
laws protecting, 50
mating, 35-37
migration, 32, 41, 43-45
miscalled "buffalo," 7, 11-12
natural enemies, 39-40
numbers of, 32, 41, 43-45, 50, 52
on currency, 22
on postage stamps, 22
photographing, 57-61
physical characteristics: coloration,
  27, 29; ears, 31; eyes, 24; hair,
  26-27; head, 29; horns, 29; hump,
  24-25, 36; mouth, 31; nose, 31;
  shedding, 27; size, 24-25; skull,
  29; speed, 24-25; strength, 25;
  tail, 24; teeth, 31; weight, 24
range, 38-40, 41
relatives of, 10
species mentioned: *Bison antiquus*,
  8; *Bison bison athabascae*, 9; *Bison bison bison*, 9; *Bison bison occidentalis*, 8-9; *Bison bonasus bonasus*, 10; *Bison bonasus caucasius*, 10; *Bison latifrons*, 8; *Bison priscus*, 8, 10
spirit buffalo, 19-20
superstitions about, 19-20

62

traits: curiosity, 33; herd activity, 32; scratching, 34; stampeding, 32; temperament, 33; wallowing, 33-34
  uses of, 19, 45-47, 55
  young, 36-37
Blackfoot, 16
Buchloe dactyloides, 37
"Buffalo Bill," 7
Buffalo Bills, 23
Buffalo Old Woman, 20
Buffalo robes, 48-50
Buffalo runners, 48

Calgary Stampede, 61
California, 41, 56
Canada, 29, 41, 44, 57, 61
Canadian Department of Agriculture, 56
Canadian Department of Indian and Northern Affairs, 55-56
Castaneda, 43
Catlin, George, 23
Cattalo, 56
Cherokee, 19
Cheyenne, 16, 46
Chipewyan, 56
Cities of Gold, 43
Clark, William, 12, 18
Cody, William F., 7
Comanche, 18
Coronado, Francisco, 43
Cortez, Hernan, 42
"Cows of the Land to the North," 43
Cree, 18, 19, 56
Creek, 19
Crow, 19, 29, 47
Custer State Park, 55, 58
Czar of Russia, 11

De Oviedo, Gonzalo, 42-43
De Vasca, Cabeza, 42
De Zaldivar, Vicente, 56

European wisent, 10-11

Florida, 41
Fort Riley, 55
Fort Smith, 55
Fox, 16

Great Buffalo, 14-15
Great Plains, 14, 34, 39, 41, 43, 50
Great White Father, 50

Hawaiian Islands, 57
Hidatsa, 16
Hide hunters, 48-50
Hornaday, William, 44

Impounding, 47-48

Jerky, 46

Kansas, 8
Kaukasus, 11
Kiowa, 15
Kutenai, 18

Lewis, Meriwether, 12
Lowland wisent, 11

Mandan, 16, 17, 18
Mississippi River, 48
Missouri River, 43
Montana, 29, 52, 58
Montezuma, 41
Mountain wisent, 10, 11

National Bison Range, 29, 52, 58
National Park Service, 55
National Zoo, 22
New Mexico, 41
New Orleans, 48
New York, 41

Pawnee, 16, 18
Pemmican, 46
"Pennsylvania buffalo," 9
Piegan, 16

63

Plains bison, 9, 23, 32, 44
Poland, 11

Rivadeneyra, Antonio, 41, 42
Russia, 8, 11

Sacred hat of the Cheyenne, 16
Saskatchewan, 44
Siberia, 8, 10
Sioux, 15, 16, 18, 20
South Dakota, 55, 58, 59
Surround, 47-48

Texas, 44

Union Pacific Railroad, 7
United States Department of the Interior, 22
Utah, 33

Wainwright Experiments, 56
"Westward Ho," 23
Wind Cave National Park, 59
Wisent, 8, 10-11, 32, 38
Wood bison, 9, 32
Wood Buffalo National Park, 55-56
Wyoming, 58

Yellowstone National Park, 50, 58

DODD, MEAD WONDERS BOOKS

Wonders of the Mosquito World by Phil Ault
Wonders of Animal Migration by Jacquelyn Berrill
Wonders of Animal Nurseries by Jacquelyn Berrill
Wonders of the Monkey World by Jacquelyn Berrill
Wonders of the Arctic by Jacquelyn Berrill
Wonders of the Fields and Ponds at Night by Jacquelyn Berrill
Wonders of the Woods and Desert at Night by Jacquelyn Berrill
Wonders of the World of Wolves by Jacquelyn Berrill
Wonders of Alligators and Crocodiles by Wyatt Blassingame
Wonders of a Kelp Forest by Joseph E. Brown
Wonders of the Pelican World by Joseph J. Cook and Ralph W. Schreiber
Wonders Inside You by Margaret Cosgrove
Wonders of the Tree World by Margaret Cosgrove
Wonders Under a Microscope by Margaret Cosgrove
Wonders of Your Senses by Margaret Cosgrove
Wonders of the Rivers by Virginia S. Eifert
Wonders Beyond the Solar System by Rocco Feravolo
Wonders of Gravity by Rocco Feravolo
Wonders of Mathematics by Rocco Feravolo
Wonders of Sound by Rocco Feravolo
Wonders of the World of the Albatross by Harvey I. and Mildred L. Fisher
Wonders of the World of Shells by Morris K. Jacobson and William K. Emerson
Wonders of Magnets and Magnetism by Owen S. Lieberg
Wonders of Measurement by Owen S. Lieberg
Wonders of Animal Architecture by Sigmund A. Lavine
Wonders of the Bat World by Sigmund A. Lavine
Wonders of the Eagle World by Sigmund A. Lavine
Wonders of the Fly World by Sigmund A. Lavine
Wonders of the Hawk World by Sigmund A. Lavine
Wonders of the World of Horses by Sigmund A. Lavine and Brigid Casey
Wonders of the Owl World by Sigmund A. Lavine
Wonders of the Spider World by Sigmund A. Lavine
Wonders of the Dinosaur World by William H. Matthews III
Wonders of Fossils by William H. Matthews III
Wonders of Sand by Christie McFall
Wonders of Snow and Ice by Christie McFall
Wonders of Stones by Christie McFall
Wonders of Gems by Richard M. Pearl
Wonders of Rocks and Minerals by Richard M. Pearl
Wonders of Barnacles by Arnold Ross and William K. Emerson
Wonders of Hummingbirds by Hilda Simon